One of the Loaves Was Yours

One of the Loaves Was Yours

JOHN J. BRUGALETTA

RESOURCE *Publications* · Eugene, Oregon

ONE OF THE LOAVES WAS YOURS

Resource Publications
An Imprint of Wipf and Stock Publishers
199 W. 8th Ave., Suite 3
Eugene, OR 97401

www.wipfandstock.com

PAPERBACK ISBN: 978-1-7252-8625-2
HARDCOVER ISBN: 978-1-7252-8626-9
EBOOK ISBN: 978-1-7252-8627-6

Manufactured in the U.S.A.   10/05/20

Contents

Acknowledgments

THE FOLLOWING POEMS WERE published in the venues indicated, occasionally with minor changes.

Faith and the Dry Times	*Anglican Theological Review*
Canonical Hours	*Lakeview Journal* (India)
Columbus	*Time of Singing*
Aquarium	*Time of Singing*
The Speed of Light	*Amethyst Review*
Hidden Design	*Mizmor Poetry Anthology*
The Edge of Light	*Radix*
Salvation Creek	*The Lyric*
Fox Sparrow	*Anglican Theological Review*

1

Other Voices

Peter Recalls the Transfiguration

I know! All you'll remember is my silly
suggestion—three booths, three tents.
I'd just woke up and still was in my dream,
the three men lit up like candles. Jeshua
brightest, yeah, but the other two "majestic"
I guess you'd say. And why not? Moses,
messenger of Law, and then Elijah, prophet.

I don't know, I must have glanced and said . . .
what foolishness I said. And then the cloud,
the Spirit's voice: "My son! Listen to him!"

Just a stupid fisherman mouthing off
about those higher things. Why can't I shut up?
I shouldn't have left my dad alone with the boat.

But how do I leave Jeshua? It would be like
saying I don't respect him. "My son"?
What does that mean? And for that matter
what does "Listen to him" mean? I listen
all the time. I wish things would be simpler.

Abel

I have a brother, older and more strict.
He bags the seed and, at the proper time,
invests it in the earth, then waits for rain.
It comes most years, but when it stays away,
he dredges and he carries but complains
that it's not fair—he followed all the rules.
And yet his way, the coaxing green from brown,
suits better what our feeble minds prefer
the world to be: stick-figures in a sketch.

With mine, the sheep and goats will not reduce
so easily to rules. I try to find
the greener grass and flowing brooks for them,
but looking does not always mean I'll find.
And even when I find, the beasts at times
will sicken and my house grow cold and still.

I've learned the best we ever do is sail
among conflicting winds and currents, blind
to most of what the world inflicts on us.
But Cain persists in making all the birds
migrate precisely on their fitting day,
the clouds arriving moist to suit his gain,
and earth lie tame, subservient to him.

We argue this, my brother (whom I love)
and I, but he can hear no words except
the echoing of his. Each time we speak,
each time we send up prayers, his anger grows.
When he decides to kill, who will be near?

Paul

I knew that darkness blocked the seeing eye,
but never that excess of light could do so too
until the day the sun itself came down
and entered in my head. It burst its light
out through my eyes and knocked me to the ground,
blind to outward circumstance, but still
a being all of light within my head.

It spoke to me, this power, so I called
it *kyrie,* for at that moment I
was so removed from who I was that I
would have addressed a locust as "my LORD."
It did not speak—and yet it did. My name
bypassed my ears and called me persecutor
of himself, as royalty would do
in speaking of his nation as himself.
I won't reiterate our words; I'll only
say the blow's own terror, the commanding
voice, my physical prostration, all
combined to shred me down to mere components.

I had now to make good sense of what
made nothing like good sense. I found
the edifice of my religion was
no building of mere stone, but held a life
within, a spirit and a voice that made
me fear for my own life and breath and sight.
This was from heaven. I could but obey.

I lived two lives, the one before the blast
and that succeeding it. But that before
was bent on cleansing obstacles that came
against my ardor for the structure I believed.
My second life removed no obstacles,
but meeting them empowered me the more.
It was the unseen part of my belief
that slapped me off my mount so, like a nut,
I could be cracked, the water trickle in,
and I could sprout and grow, not rot and die.

Instead of accolades for bringing bound
believers in to see them stoned to death,
I found myself extolling love, the kind
that sees a use in differences, that makes
one's love for hotheads just as warm as for
judicious silence or the meek of heart.

Cleopas

Luke 24:13

How could he have been captured through deceit?
We'd walked with him, my wife and I, and saw
his quick detection of a foe's device.
What happened must have been enchantment by
satanic guile. Or was it heavenly?

He was our fervent hope's embodiment,
and hope so high may fall disastrously.
We tried to tell this to the Stranger on
the road toward home, to which He listened, then
this Slave (we saw the stripes his whipping gave)
schooled us in Scripture's having planned it all.

He broke the bread with us as if he were
the master of the house; and prayed in just
the way the LORD had done. We both were then
about to shout our recognition when
he turned to empty air. Was this another
fragile hope? Ah me, how can one tell?

But hope of any kind is rare for us.
And when it stares one in the face, you know
there's truly something better than despair.

Agape Champion

What insolence, to ask if I can love.
Of all those you might ask, you come to me?
I, who teach it others by the way
I live, my arms spread wide for that embrace
the sage apostle said to give our friends.
My face will ache when I relax at home,
the thorn that follows days of rosy smiles.

And everyone I love I then forgive,
and then forgive again when they return
my love with snide remarks and filth in words.
Four hundred ninety times the LORD commands
we wipe remembering's painful slate of those
offending us. My worst offender gave
two hundred forty-two. I still forgive.

I would not like to think of his demise,
the boiling pitch up to his nether parts,
huge hornets stinging lips and eyes, the roar
of locomotives always in his ears.
No, I should like to see him smiling when
at last he sees the love that passed him by.
It's that I pray for, that I beg to see.

Assuming you're aware my Emma's gone,
you must have heard how loud I wept.
She cooked, she cleaned. It's true she criticized,
but that's all right. I grinned and shrugged it off.
I hardly think of it these days at all.
I wept for love, and just before she went,
I said to smile and took her photograph.

I made her happy, that much I can prove.
Her smile reflected love I always gave.

Eve

It was a kind of leisure there to prune
and dig without undue exertion's sweat.
We idly played the gardeners, but work
had none of its contemporary ache.
I severed here a twig, while Adam stood
a pair of steps away to loose the loam.

It was the gleaming snake ensnarled in trees
that made me look more close than I had done.
I thought I heard the steps of Yahweh's feet,
but it was nothing but the blowing leaves.
Besides, the day was not of age for walking.

I looked again and saw the viper stare,
then spread its lips, then speak, unlike a beast:

I think you've only now examined things
with care, the way adults will see and judge.
What magic has lent focus to your eyes?

I didn't know and asked him what he knew.

I know the things that Yahweh has forbidden—
the silent thoughts of others, water's way
with stone, and what authority has placed
in plainest view like other trees, and yet
has banned. Is it not true this tree is banned?

It's true, yet I had thought . . . How did you know?

The way I know that you're an infant girl
and not a woman; by your nakedness.
You and your cohort think yourselves pleased
by merely following the rule laid down,
despite the tree's displaying in your view,
and that so boldly it negates the rule.

His thoughts were convoluted as his form.
My head began to ache. Simplicity
was what I longed for, to slice through his words.
Would leaves about me satisfy critiques?
Not if my childishness was at the core
and not periphery of me. Enough
details. I ate. The concepts were a deluge.
I shared the news with Adam, lest I have
a suckling boy for husband. Then we both
began a life of seeing things up close:
the snarl of evil, peace and love of good;
the guiding nimbus of maturity,
the painfulness of growing to be wise.

I wonder would I make the choice again?
And was that leafy rustle Yahweh's breath?
Was he observing his design's collapse,
or was it blossoming as he had planned?
All I know for certain is there can
be too much leisure, too much relaxation.

Simon the Magician

I fail to understand the hatred some
have spat at those of us who long to wield
a power greater than the run of men.
Are none to be admired by gaping mouths?
What pleasure in a life when no one does
the seemingly impossible, a lamb
become a fox, a jar of wheat now sand,
a newborn daughter changed to nanny goat?
These things give flavor like a pinch of salt.

The poor Samaritans, astonished, gave
me silver to enact my magic tricks.
My cunning pleased them mightily, and they
accorded me a might that pleased myself.
Was this not a fair exchange we made?
To walk the roads and with a scowl make cringe
the man who heretofore had led the town,
or smile at adolescent girls and see
obeisance in their eyes, all this and more
was paradise to me till fortune turned
and Philip's tricks outdid mine in their eyes.
I thought it cautious to blend in with him
and learn what joyed the rabble overmuch.
His differed subtly, so it took some days.

I cannot tell a lie—it baffled me.

Then came their finest sort: two fishermen,
who told the crowd, "Receive the holy spirit."
I'd never met a spirit with the smallest
part of holiness, and doubted such.
But these Samaritans, these surly oafs,
these cheats, these trite believing fools transformed
to bleating sheep, embracing men they'd known
to rob them and accuse them of such acts
as Cain could not perform. I knew their wine
or bread was drugged, but with no drug I knew.

I'd heard of Judas, who'd received a bag
of silver and was cursed for taking it.
I would reverse his fault and give them some
to merely know the potion's name and source.
But nothing I could do, no action
done in friendship and in innocence
could gain me entry to their stiff cabal.
I thought it best to leave in peace, so made
a final gesture of goodwill, to shame
the prigs for coldly ostracizing me.
I bid them pray for me and left them with
their hands up high as if their god could soar
and would, at their request, drop something white.

One of the Loaves Was His

Do you not yet understand or remember the
five loaves of the five thousand? Matthew 16:9

One of the little loaves was mine,
a lunch for body while my soul
would feed on what the rabbi said.
His follower demanded it,
and I, a boy, gave my consent.

But soon concern for stomach left.
They'd gathered four to add to mine
and two small fish—a pittance for
the thousands who would miss a meal.

And then the thousands could not eat
that multitude of loaves and fish.
But where had they acquired them all?
And why so much more than the need?

I pondered this for weeks to come.
That's when my thinking took a turn:
His words had not remained with me,
but everything he did came back—
his blessing of the meager food;
assigning his disciples work;
the fact that those who had should give
the small amount they had on them.

The lesson, I soon saw, was in
the actions with the spoken words.
They said, "No matter what the means
at our disposal, it will be
enough and more when God assists
our utmost in attending his
adoptive family on earth."

It helps me, now I am a man,
to feel my tiny gift will make
a difference in the world, and me.

Breakfast with Him

I heard him get up and go out in the dark.
The scent of him grew fainter in the house.
He walked until I couldn't hear, or else he stopped.

Soon I felt a little stomach pang, like puppy love.
I knew then he was praying—back and forth.
It seemed like days till he returned, but hardly dawn.

I saw him enter only when I looked aside of him.
I was about to offer him some fruit to eat.
Something made me shy, the moment's fulcrum maybe.

So he asked me, and I took minutes to accept.
I almost took too long—thank God I spoke.
It seemed a sacrilege to not be serving Him.

But then at least there was some give-and-take.
I think of him a lot when I can't sleep, miss him a lot.

Columbus

I thought it was the East when I had landed.
It took awhile to see the earth expanded—
this seeming-flat and shrunken disk as globe
that Christians will envelop like a robe.

The Northerners had found the place before,
which, if it's true, might make my smelly chore
seem futile, but I'm not sure that it does.
Their concept of the earth stayed what it was.

Perhaps because they lacked Balboa's shock,
that came to him while perched upon a rock
and seeing yet another ocean's mass
as like the first as in a looking glass.

But what I meant to say was "east is west"
is true, as I had proved and not a jest.
It only needs abandoning some rules
the way we leave behind our grammar schools.

For what is round will always come around
and take us to all heaven's base and ground.
I did not sail for spices or for gold,
but for the promised land that was foretold.

The Lawyer

Luke 10:23ff.

We officials discussed the man who said he came
from heaven, the blasphemy of it, reversing
all we knew—that some go, not come from there.

When he was wandering nearby, I accosted him.
"Rabbi," I began, just to soften his suspicions,
"what shall I do to inherit eternal life?"

He asked me what the Law says, and I replied,
"Love God, etcetera, and love your neighbor."
This he approved: "Do this and you will live."

My first try fallen limp, I righted myself and asked,
"Who is my neighbor?" I knew this would cut him.
But no, I got one of his tales. This one posited

two Jews who left a robbed and injured man to die,
then a Samaritan who wined and oiled his wounds,
and all the rest of it. Then he questioned me,

"Which of the three was neighbor to the man?"
I'd heard of his healings and his promises,
as well as his caring for Romans and Samaritans,

so I understood he wore the Samaritan's' cloak.
But I could not say, "You are." All I could say
was, "The one who demonstrated compassion."

I hated him more than ever for disturbing
the settled contract I had had under the Law—
for demanding what I could never muster.

Love a Samaritan? What next, become one?

The Serpent

Because he did not tell me, ordered not
that my mouth should avoid one single tree,
its scented and most promising-sweet fruit,
I slid along and flicked a tongueful of
its redolence. It pleased. I swallowed it.
The shadows having moved (a little moved),
I tasted it, the savor sliding through
and permeating me with piquancy.
I coiled and coiled some more to sleep it off.

What dreams I dreamt. I will not say what dreams
passed into me, but I was colonized.
Not instantaneous, but clarity,
or something like it, granted entrance of
my eyes into the mute interstices.
And with this probity, this knowing, came,
as hide with hyrax, rider of my will,
immersed my face into unquarried stone.
I was engulfed by what I had engulfed.

I saw the chaos, saw his moving Mind,
the dark recoiling as his light advanced,
and a progressive sorting, ordering.
This made no sense; the chaos had been wild,
a flustering exuberance that raced
the pulse. To housebreak this dissatisfied.

And then he shaped an upright form, in spite,
I think, of my designed recumbent one,
and gave to them a cognizance akin,
if somewhat yet unformed, to his. It fit.
The framework and the tidiness comprised
a suitable terrarium, a nest,
a cozy crib, a haven for a child.

That I was so employed, when I was led
to lead them to abandon infancy,
to give tranquility for intellect,
for knowing what is his and what is not,
I am by turns both proud and much abashed.
I know some portion, as they know some parts,
but if my rider was in league with him,
or merely vandal, I wish not to know.

2

Prayers

Praying

To kneel or lie down prone and speak
with no one else nearby is droll
if You are not much interested,
or worse, if You do not exist.

But I go on with what today
would seem to be a fine charade,
a talking to a part of me
that knows how curious it is
to ask insensate walls for help.

And why do so? I think because
there is some chance that You are there
and listening. And if that's so,
You are not one that I would shun.

So once again I ink my thoughts,
crumple the note around a stone
and throw it out into salt waves.

No reply is needed, I would guess.
If we ever meet, I won't mention it.
I'll just wait for You to bring it up.

Willfulness

Be not so dainty over my free will,
but if You grant my current prayer, I beg
that You then make my will like your own;
for I have seen insanities we make
when "Freedom" is their call, and chaos comes.

Let me be free to choose, and I might pick
the coarsest knave, the dullest simpleton
to lead me in response to love of home,
or in response to what my homeland was,
or even in nostalgia's mindless grip.

Give me, give *us,* the wisdom You possess,
But not in full, I plead. Our minds cannot
enfold what nestles in your own. Take care
that our thin skulls do not explode in zeal
to be as You, which was our fall's one cause.

Acid

I told You yesterday, Omnipotence,
I'd give you glory with those hammered words.
I lied. And You sat listening, amused
that one should offer, think the task was done,
and then return to stealing from his God.

Which limb is it that I must amputate,
what glossy organ pluck, from which this pride
secretes like acid to erode my life?
You know, and you alone possess the skill
to pull it, roots and all, and leave behind
this fond, distorted etching of your face.

Repentance at Its Work

You have seen fit, now that I have confessed,
to smile on me and make me one who's blest
with wife and son, with those who like good work.
You have released me from my major quirk,
my lifelong sickness, lawless in your eyes.

You've saved me from a thousand deaths and lies
that You, with perfect justice, could despise.
But Perfect Love has triumphed and I live
forgiven and obliged to then forgive.

Direct my pen, O God, and let my will
be modeled onto yours. Let me be still
and listen when I pray, that I may hear
your counsel. Leave my conscience clear.

Prayer for Steadfastness

My LORD, it's manifest that I grow old,
and yet You bless me so that I am bold
to beg you teach me of what's right.

I walk unsteadily and think of You
at rare (at gemlike) moments all too few.
I dare not ask your full insight,

but I would wed the just and merciful
like arms that can both push and pull.
Let me, a cell, obey your Mind,

so that I will, with wanting cells like me,
be bound with them, to You, and so be free.
Give me your firmness to be kind.

Prayer III

Father, I am glum today.
Send these pesky clouds away.
I don't mean the ones that rain.

I mean those that will detain
my impulse to send a card
to a friend who finds it hard
in this life to wash and eat.

Also those who cannot meet
large expenses that arrive
every month while we're alive.

Give me something to revive
what had been my daily bliss.

Wait! I think I've gone amiss.
Now that I have truly prayed,
I'm no longer so afraid
that I've lost the Spirit's gift.

Thank you, LORD. Your love will lift
even sodden hearts to bloom
in the saddest lonely room.

Prayer for Those Ill and Wounded

Here you lie in bed and waiting
for the doctor's daily round.
In the meantime we're consulting
greatest of all healers found.

LORD you cured the blind and crippled.
Heal today this godly child.
Accidents and all diseases
You will tame that once were wild.

Comfort if You please, LORD Jesus
all the sick and those in pain.
Give the doctors holy wisdom.
Let their faith not be in vain.

A Plea for Wisdom

Let me not ever utter yes to lies,
to pious fictions that engender hope.
I would not wring truth's neck until its eyes
remit their witness in the telescope.

But let me neither stop my ears because
a story lays a basis for my peace.
We sniff when uncles quote their well-worn saws,
but use makes no validity decrease.

Give me such wisdom as to know by touch
a fabrication from a bedrock fact.
And if this last request is not too much,
add courage to relay such truths intact.

Though faith ignores the sense, and blind men see,
A sweet lie's fetid when two fools agree.

For the Restoration of the Church

Forgive us, God, the trifles of our rites,
our crooning of clichés, our comfort in
the lackadaisical routine of praise,
our mumbling creeds while thinking of our clothes,
our hawking of a faith we lightly chose.
We cling to these because all else seems wild,
and quicker acts would hint of brutish scenes.

When You told Moses he must bare his feet,
he no doubt understood he was a slave
before the Presence of your blazing lips.
Shock us, great LORD, into a creature's mind,
a mind like his, subservient and meek,
an act of courage in predation's world.
Prune off the proud excrescences we love,
that we may gather at your feet and ask
no more except that You receive our awe.
Then we will truly worship and be yours.

Just as in heaven there will be no Book,
no church exists where everywhere is church.
We have not grown enough, perhaps, to voice
our pillow talk with such a nakedness,
but we can steel our nerves to edge toward
some semblance of your willing slave's delight.

Ash Wednesday

(To be read aloud in private)

For things I've done or left undone, I lament.
For praising insincerely, I'm contrite.
For blaspheming for laughter, I repent.
For blaming others wrongly, I regret.
For my prevarications, I'm aggrieved.
For passing rumors on, I wish undone.
For leaving gifts unlauded, I'm red-faced.
For envying the rich, I am abashed.
For setting traps, I am compunctious.
For seeking compliments, I am abject.

For these and more, I wear a cross of dust
for it's from dust that I was made, and then
when dead all dust my body will become.
Forgive the many ways in which I've strayed.

Prayer for the Parousia

LORD, I am concerned about your Word.
How can we believe all that it says?
It's in a leaky boat. The bilge is smearing
whatever had been told and written in
a trusted ink. For some had wished it changed.

The soldier's javelin with sponge and wine
became the feeble hyssop's inept stem.
Judas hanged himself—or did he leap
from some high cliff to death by suicide?
Were Moses and Elijah glorified
with Christ, or was their radiance much less?
And then poor Junia was made a man
because she's listed as apostle, therefore male.

On this termited platform we are urged
to base our faith because there is no other.
Lies indeed infect the Word of truth
until the honest miracles are deemed
prevarications by dishonest fools
who build their glory on their prejudice.

Come, LORD Christ, and bring your knotted cords
to cleanse the desecration of your Word.

Careful Infinity

Our minds tell us that you are near;
our hearts feel you are far away.

When you were here we saw you eat;
you used a cushion on a boat.
Your flesh was tender, like our own.
And so the thorns, the nails and spear
tore what the floggings left untorn.

Your distance since that fatal day,
when you both ate and disappeared,
will say you're now invisible
but at our shoulder as we walk.

You are both near and far away,
for we sometimes detect your will
as we might sense our neighbor's grin,
but we're protected from the sin
of placing fleshly pain on you.

Great careful LORD, our gratitude
is as inadequate as string
would be to measure outer space
or circumvent infinity.

Prayer for the Golden Age

Bestowing peace upon our frightened head,
You made it clear that peace within our chest
was what You meant, and not this world of lead.
For worldly peace was left to be our quest,

a troubled search as for a golden age
ahead and none behind. Two phases then.
Show us, good LORD, how we may disengage
our fright for vipers with our calm "Amen."

Are we the seed to be somehow refined,
then eaten by this predatory world?
It is a process that *does* seem aligned
with that tight start from which our space unfurled.

If this is your own plan, then may it be.
Steel us to step where we can hardly see.

Plague

We're here my LORD and waiting for your will.
Our lives on earth are in your regal hands
like water that may trickle to the sea
and lose itself in superfluity.

Yet some have turned away from twisted lives,
repenting their esteem for bogus gods,
for thrills or money, power over others.
Will You not firm your hands so they'll know You?

We're told that You will take the least occasion
to demonstrate your mercy. This we believe.
Help us to believe it when we die.

Nutrient-Rich Loam

Make my soul a fertile ground
for your word's intent profound.
Let it send its roots so deep
that I may not soundly sleep.
Let it send up shoots and bear
fruit of understanding care.

I don't ask to be unique;
none could care and also seek
to surpass his siblings' gift.
All I ask is that You lift
my bare spirit from the mire
so that I might play the lyre
and produce what may festoon
every midnight till it's noon.

Then when all sing in your choir,
let us never ever tire
of producing lyric songs
for the One to whom belongs
all for which my spirit longs.

3

Uplifting

Blessings

When I was young, I wanted to be blessed
with approbation for my being there.
And failing that, for passing one small test:
a mended chair, or just for playing fair.

Now that I'm old, my blessing is to bless
whatever goodness in the world I'll find:
her knowing guess, my enemy's success,
or any act or word that's true and kind.

Ragged Robin

You gardeners who grow those hybrid teas—
unless subsisting on their own frail roots,
piteous wraiths producing bloodless blooms—
they're powered by a rootstock out of sight.

It's down below, their winter self reversed,
that Ragged Robin, unremarkable
in flowering, but avid in submission
to the soil, sends beauty to your sight.

And you, resplendent in your graceful walk,
that tulip glass of Pinot Noir you lift—
what Being, lopped and grafted, feeds your life?

What loving self-denial raises you
above the quadrupeds so that your face
with ease can see the lightning and the stars?

The Easter Victory

Messiahs came, messiahs died;
till yet another One brought hope,
but seemed to fail as well when he was killed.

And yet three days entombed and God
had raised him from the grave to speak,
to show his wounds, to eat a piece of fish.

Now who but God, who made us all,
could wake the one who pleased him most?
By dying, mind you, not by winning wars.

Not petty wars with soldiers but
by overcoming death to save us all
from that one thing we fear the most: to die.

But now that we are told of this
and call it "Resurrection's gift,"
some lip the word yet leave the act behind.

But we break out the colored eggs
and rabbits which we hope will mean
that life comes back for those who love the LORD.

A Healing

We tried a different church one Sunday.
The altar was surrounded by the pews
which I concluded was a novelty
that I could do without. The sermon started.

It too was novel, though on a kind of prayer.
The rector soon went silent. We were to pray
for something or someone, and then to wait
and listen—for a "still, small voice" perhaps.

It changed my life. It was neither still
nor small. I'd prayed that our annoying son
would grow to be humane and civilized.
I heard a voice say, "I will take care of him."

It wasn't long before our son was healed.
He had become humane and civilized.

The Garden Within

Having cleared a weedy square of yard,
I bought assorted, high-priced garden seeds
and sowed them in the straightest lines I could.
Then soaking them, I left them to the sun.

I thought my job was done, and I would pick
tomatoes, lettuce, radishes and corn.
But it surprised me when they sprouted as
oxalis, spurge, colewort, nettle, dock.

I had not thought the weeds would leave their seeds,
but up they came and choked the plants I sowed.
When spring returned I did it all again.
This time I tried to sift what weeds had left.

Once more the weeds came up and spoiled my crop.
I fell back on my faith and prayed to God
that he would help me cleanse my garden plot.
He said, "Those weeds are growing in your soul.
Repent sincerely for your life to heal."

Hidden Design

Is there order in this untamed world?
Not in garden borders, nor in clipped
resemblance of a rabbit or a dog,
but in the form the plant itself obeys.

For example, leaves around a stem
that rises through the center of the plant
will follow Fibonacci's theorem:
one and one and three, then five and eight.

There is some order that we do not see
because it's hidden from our eyes and minds
by wide adaptions to the climate zones.
But still we have not answered how

this neat arrangement settled in our plants.
Ingenious horticulturists did not
exist when plants evolved into themselves.
It's so precise, there must have been a Mind.

Love vs. Salvation

Rugosa is a rugged kind of rose.
It shrugs off mildew and it stares down deer,
but this one wouldn't grow and so
I moved it where it had a lot more sun
and watered it and fed it mild amounts.

I love its old-man leaves,
its baby-finger blossoms,
its hips like cherries in the fall.

Though others grew and spread,
this one died.
Despite my tending and my love,
some quirk within it snuffed its will
to carry out inherited design.

I'm sincerely sorry.
But when I've tried all possibilities,
it goes to compost,
leaving soil and sun for other things to grow.

Emptied for Blessings

Glory be to God for plans that fail,
for races lost and fish that got away,
broken knives, friendships soured, wrecks,
for fiancees who married someone else.

Praise him for the gullied face, the fat,
the burgled house now violated trash,
road-map legs, mustache, crow's feet,
the veteran's stubborn nightmares.

What else could show how empty life can be
when faithful spouse, loving children, wealth
and jolts of joy will jade us like good health?

We are mere children, we who are of age,
not calling until lack of means to pay
force us to the floor, sobbing, praying.

With the Savior

Without the Christ, what would this life be like?
A darkened room, no windows and no door.
The senseless repetition of a chore.
An ocean's flood without a hill or dike.

No stars or moon; an endless, pointless hike;
an evil tyrant spreading blood and gore;
all interests and pleasures just a bore;
each blade of grass as piercing as a pike.

Yet now we've heard a loving father rules,
benevolent enough to make worthwhile
our foolish leaders and our dying star.

We tolerate our neighbors and their guile,
and smoke the recent father's cheap cigar
with wisdom's patience and its hallmark smile.

Pascal's Wager

We've heard the wager that Pascal set up
that always wins for those who shun God's cup,
who feel they cannot easily decide
whether to believe or "let it ride."

He said, "Believe. If God is there, you've won;
and if He isn't there, what harm is done?"
But there's a problem that we all can see:
Is God a horse, and are his creatures free
to bet on whether he can be or not?
"Just do the math." How crass. What rot!

Would we so bet on if our spouse is true?
What friendship can be based on such a clue
as lack of proof? Would God be witness in
our courtroom if our only way to win
is to believe him when he says, "I Am?"

I'm sure the mathematician thought it well
to save a lot of skeptics from their hell,
but those so "saved" may not be those whom He,
in giving us free will, will not agree.

Beware to trifle with the Holy One
who made the galaxies and our warm sun.

The Speed of Light

A billion light years is a fantasy
to me and to a lot of other folks.
It ripples off the tongue like *meet for tea*
and lots of other phrases, even jokes.

But try to think of it in miles or feet.
How many trips to board a cruise?
That speed your shot goes in a game of skeet—
the pellets are not fast at all. They ooze.

Before and after all our lives, the stars
explode, black holes collide and spread in trillions
while we eat breakfast, read a book, drive cars.
We live our tiny lives in modest millions.

Yet we, and maybe only we, observe
and think of it. Is that the way we serve?

Salvation Creek

These woods are dusty in July,
and August too; they're both so dry.

A man could die of thirst out here,
although it seems to suit the deer.

No house nearby, but down a slope
where water ran there may be hope

of rope-sized rivulet to drink,
to slake my thirst and try to think.

I blink; the trees have lost their charm;
mosquitoes feast on either arm.

Unease alarms my bosky stroll,
which was my morning's early goal.

I envy every mole's retreat
away from sun's infernal heat,

whose meat and drink is worm and root,
whose life's conservative and mute.

I hear a hoot. Athena's bird.
She may be wise . . . what's that? Absurd.

A purling creek! That's what I heard.

Easter

It's common knowledge, dead men don't return,
but common knowledge isn't always true.
There is one case that most still have to learn.

He rose (not for revenge), the one they slew
and left the door ajar to heaven's table
for those who lastly honored his small crew.

It's so unnatural that it's no fable
but huge life in another (fifth?) dimension,
a better home beneath a better gable.

It's there for mere belief, though not pretension,
belief that manifests itself in love
which always will demand one's full attention.

It's not for sale, but fits us like a glove,
free as the wind or as a mourning dove.

Dying Stars

Those gazers at the stars, our modern magi,
have seen and meditated on and then
conceived the source of short-lived gamma bursts:
each is some star's implosive death that spreads
its dying to all forms of life nearby.

Each day the news arrives: another world
of tyrants, politicians, widows, pets
has vanished in the time it takes to blink.
One happened ninety-billion years ago;
like distance, time is different with the stars.

And we who watch these pallid news reports
begin to see how dangerous it is
to live amid such overwhelming deaths—
begin to see how coddled we may be
to have survived the little time we have.

As You Love Yourself

Not only do we instinctively reach for
the strawberries others might have wished for,
but even more importantly, when friends
misunderstand our motives, or mistakenly
suspect us of scheming, we hug to ourselves
the better story, supposing there to be one.

We sometimes think, *God sees this, and one day*
they will too, and all will be well. Well, well!
And do you suppose we are the only ones who are
misinterpreted, given no benefit of the doubt,
automatically ascribed the worst of motivations?

Brothers and sisters in the faith we call them
because we share their DNA, their deformations
and their kindnesses, their inscrutability.
If we could be reading them amiss, we have
a prescription for our ailment: Pretend for a
moment or two, just for a moment, they are you.

How to Think about God

One: Tell yourself you are able to do it.
After all, you are *homo sapiens,* a knowing
human being.

Two: You discard the bearded old man, the
bright blur, and the strong black woman.

Three: You are left with nothing, a void, so
you think about that. But it's too frightening
to last.

Four: Then you remember your favorite
teacher: widely read, able to discuss any
topic, kind, ethical. But you recall a flaw:
he or she smoked.

Five: You turn to nature, the tamed kind of
course. Or money. Take care with the
predators. Yet they save you from
panentheism.

Six: You strive to become more sensitive,
more tactful, more welcoming. So
children fling stones at you, former
friends pretend they don't see you, your
wife invites her boyfriends in for the
night.

Seven: On the last day of your life, you
rest from your exertions, and he comes
to you.

By the Light

I see by the light of the risen sun
a flock of laying hens, children at their play,
the playwright sitting at an oaken desk,
teachers making lesson plans, families
at their evening meals, and more, much more.

And by the light of Christianity
I see a man in his car passing a young woman
hitch-hiking. He turns his car around,
invites her to the passenger seat,
and takes her to a motel where he pays the fee,
and then goes home, faithful to his wife.

I see drivers giving jump-starts,
women making meals for the housebound,
elders sewing face masks for physicians,
all of them while praying for strangers.

Angling for Love

It's like a man who thinks he maybe has
a very little chance of wedding her,
but woos her nonetheless, then sees that she
was angling for his eye, which made him love.

A lot like that, we suddenly begin
to wonder if there isn't something in
religion after all, so start to read the
Koran, Upanishads, and then at last
the Bible. We read it like a novel then,
like a single book, and tire of the begats,
so turn to what we're sure is a translation.

Once there, the gospels. That's when we were caught.
But caught by what? An angler, that is clear.
By Mark or Matthew, Luke or John? Perhaps.
But who caught them? A greater Angler I suppose.

4

Inconveniences

The Edge of Light

A clearing in old growth,
a campfire at its hub,
our tents pitched all around
along the edge of light.
We lay in sleeping bags,
some telling tales
to push the dawning near
the threat of darkened woods.

The stories went around
until we mostly were
agreed that some had shed
new light upon the fire—
redundancy at best.
Some lay along the edge,
while others went too far
into the baffling dark
for us to understand,
and so brought in more dark.

We've moved our tents away
at almost every dusk
to know more of what used
to be the trackless dark.
But some still love the dark
because it seems to them
that it will make them free.
We've had no word from them,
only their gargled pleas.

A Brief History of Eternity

Having sensed a master behind the birth of stars
and the complexity of epigenomes, the people were
in awe both of his immensity and his undetectability.
Now and then one of them dared to imagine a human
conversing with him, bargaining, even quarreling.
These were more effective for their impossibility.

When he showed up, it was as if Apollo had been born
to a bowyer's wife, a neighbor of yours, but no favorite.
His mother had a wild tale of Hermes talking to her,
but we all assumed a Thracian in the woodpile.
Yet he said he is, and He would not stay dead.
Finally we decided it was the best way to explain his puzzle.

And then it wasn't long before we'd grown used to him,
to his titles, his impossible actions, his odd mixture
of gentleness and huge demands; to his utterly foreign
view of life in which meekness wins and grief is happiness.
All of these astounding things we had found words for,
and having found them, put the things in a cupboard forever.

Pentecost

Each of them had a tongue of light above his head,
and the tongue was divided, like the healing snake's.
The tongue of each spoke two languages, his own
and that of a foreign group: Medes and Lutherans,
Parthians and Baptists, Cretans and Presbyterians,
Catholics and Orthodox, Quakers and Arians.

All of the apostles spoke the Word of God,
but each of the groups heard it as their jargon.
The fresh Word, free of the growths of factionalism,
rang true in each of them as the original facts
upon which their dissensions had accreted,
bearing quandaries like "real presence" or "memorial,"
a trivial dividing of memory's power to awaken the past.

It revealed the question of clerical garb to be one of
the degree of authority allowed to clergy over laity,
a matter of preference arising out of culture and family.
Infant baptism or adult, immersion or sprinkling,
prescribed prayers or impromptu, kneeling or slouching,
all to be sanded away by a common cause; not an enemy
but an overpowering gratitude, eventually forming love.

Easter II

Who would believe that time can be reversed,
that youth's reclaimable, and more,
that what we were at first
may be improved to what we held as spore?

Such is this stark impossibility—
so free of reason that we name
it, making it less free,
for God is wild and we prefer him tame.

We call it *Resurrection* and thereby
pretend we've mastered all it is,
which is, of course, a lie:
Our minds and hearts are not the likes of his.

When faced with what we cannot comprehend,
give us the courage, gracious Lord,
to let our heads descend
and learn our souls and minds have soared.

A Theocracy?

When tempted in the desert
he rejected power over cities.
And when people tried to make him king,
he took himself away.

He seemed to see something untimely
about a theocracy,
but what could have been misguided
about the opinions of both Satan and people?

Surely rule by a Christian government
would adhere to Christian principles,
don't you think?

Yet he did not.

Perhaps, just perhaps,
it had something to do with his opinion
that even heaven-sent things
are sullied by us.

The Problem of Pain

Ah theodicy, what a hard sell you are
with your many-headed versions on the shelves:
Augustine, Irenaeus, Thomas Aquinas,
Leibniz, Voltaire and John Hick;
all of them ignored by those who vote
according to their feelings and their scars.

Those who step back a moment from their
resentments, however, should attend to
the many adjustments made to our universe,
all of them together allowing for life.

What sort of world would we desire?
Would it be a world without death, wars,
or winter's freezing inconveniences?
One where dessert leaps into mouths
and suffice for health? How would that produce
the Sistine ceiling, children's learning,
music and civilization? Do we yearn to be
pampered imbeciles on a tropical island
where might makes right, and everyone
is a king or a queen over no one?

Or does complaining about God
make us feel erudite and compassionate?

Maturing

Each day means fewer things that he can do.
Some years ago he lost his sense of smell,
and now he hardly bends to tie his shoe.

You understand. I'm sure that you can tell
he's getting old; he's edging toward his grave.
Slave traders aren't enticed. He wouldn't sell.

I won't say he is cowardly or brave—
he's just uninterested in pain or fear.
He's lived from birth inside a verbal cave.

But now his heart is wrung, his eyes are blear,
and he has seen some things he'll never say,
except by tangents, from this biosphere.

One thing he still delights in is to play
while kneeling with a child as if he'd pray.

Praying or Playing?

When I have fallen out of love with time,
my food like water from a stagnant pond,
my taste for poetry gone dull or nil,
and my delights diminished to a rhyme,

I think of him from whom I've had reply.
But none today. None, though I've cast myself
prostrate and begged of him new life for me.
Ah, now I see. It is an empty sky.

But no. When he sojourned with us, he died
with arms spread wide as if he would embrace
us all, those downcast or those dignified.

My abject body did not worship him.
I was an actor begging his belief,
so praying for myself was soft and dim.

Strange Words

I knew a man who called his trying day
"a day from heck." Now God is baffled,
I am sure, as to what the word heck means.

Certainly it can't mean hell, for God forbids
the pronouncing of that word. That's why
there are scant dozens of mentions in
his Bible, 21 in the New Testament alone.

So I am puzzled by certain Christians who say
darn, shoot, phooey, by golly and goshdarned,
as puzzled, I suppose, as the Everlasting is.

A Refusal to Mourn

How can I mourn those blazoned dead
who now reside in the orbiting light,
their leavings a handful of ash, a wisp of gas or a name?

Who is worthy to stand in the glare
of their lives' collapse who would not have boarded
a bulleting plane for the chance to shunt it aside?

What would I say of those who refused
to disown our visiting God, who embraced
the fangs and flames as friends who would lead them home?

All that is sure of the dead we knew
is they woke in the morning and went to work
and never again went to bed.

Now and again everyday acts become parabolic,
telling perhaps how one day the king will return
when everyone living is doing his usual chores.

Choices

When will we know if we have chosen well?
Were ancients right; are fates controlled by stars?
Or is there Mind and Heart that made those orbs,
and are we given freedom to decide?
We do not know—we may not ever know,
but we believe, which is to say we trust,
the way we trust a soul-mate to be true.

It's like our trusting that the world will last
when civil systems shatter in a day,
or plagues destroy our families and friends.

We have the beds we made, we lie in them,
and though they feel like stones, we try to sleep.
If images of bliss wake us at night,
we don't reject them as the devil's bait,
but offer thanks for such exceeding love.

December/May

When David lay without enthusiasm
on his wide mattress chill and powerless,
physicians thought a touch of youth's new heat
would fill with lifeblood his shrunk limbs.

They scanned the nubile gamines of his realm
and opted for a girl named Abishag,
a plump and roseate, a tender girl,
sixteen, perhaps a year or two beyond,
who blushed when looked on, giggled every word.

The doctors saw in her a poultice and
applied her to the king to draw from him
the imp or demon that was parasite.

She drew instead (unknown to her, poor child)
what little life remained, not through his lust,
but through his wounding recognition that
all that was ended, and with that, his life.

Estate Sale

Seven short-wave radios (best that were sold in their time),
a table saw (used once when new, rusted today),
ranks and orders of shoes, boots, slippers, and clogs,
a regiment of tools, devices, machines
for clipping, tilling, blending, pounding, and coating,
all on display in the yard for a price, like servants
acquired to impress, ignored, now bared to the crowd,
naked to view in the searching, unpitying sunlight.

In an unregarded corner stands a man,
sorrowful and looking at nothing, it seems, at the ground,
looking as if this were not the only grief he has had.
A relation, surely, his face marred beyond recognition.
The bargain hunters avoid acknowledging him,
thinking perhaps he would dampen their fun in the picking.
For whom does he grieve? The dead in their graves
or the upright ones always devouring, always starving?

Discernment

The preacher's sermon's long. Then from the back
a child drowns out his every other word.
The pious are disturbed by her loud howls
and liken them to those condemned to hell,
while others who remember Paul's harangue
will secretly applaud the child's critique.

It makes a question: Which of them performs
the work of God and which does not?
It seems so simple to applaud the church,
but we've been wrong so many times before.

The Meaning of Our Life

What am I? I am myself a word spoken by God.
Can God speak a word that does not have any meaning?
THOMAS MERTON

And what, pray tell, is that meaning for us?
Is it one that he intended at our beginning?
One that he laid on us from our skin inward?
Or does he instill it in the core of our being,
then encourages it to develop outward,
manifesting itself in our loving lives?

That is, does he cultivate it by rules, and
relationships? Or are we to create our own
meaning from within, doing this together
with God in his grace? Is our meaning to be
one that reflects his will and makes us his
word spoken freely as if we made it alone?

Just who and what we are sits hidden in
God's endowing us with freedom, as well
as in our courageous response to that
endowment.

We will never discover the purpose and
meaning of our lives if we only try to escape
the fear brought upon us by our first
encounter with our seeming lack of meaning.

The Wedding Feast at Cana

Although it covers one entire wall,
the guests and hangers-on spill out the sides,
for Veronese could not make it hold
the great, unruly number who, with Christ
in hearing, still would prattle of the food,
the chance of rain, migrating birds, or tell
the story of a bunion's agony.

They are, of course, not tipsy by this time,
the host just tasting what a wine should be.
So no one's had a drink when we allow
whole days to be consumed with choosing clothes,
or training grass to do a carpet's job,
while somewhere in the house there sits the man
who stares unheeded deep within our eyes.

Processional Hymn

Here we come, our Lord and Savior,
    Back to hear your word once more.
That's enough of misbehavior;
    We're a little sad and sore.

We will change our thoughts and actions
    If you'll give us one more chance.
We'll clean up our interactions
    And assume a Christian stance.

We've been gone so long and we're so
    Happy now to have returned;
And we're glad that you are near so
    Maybe now we won't be burned.

We're not hungry; please don't trouble;
    Just a taste of wine and bread.
After grazing worldly stubble,
    Yours becomes a festive spread.

We're not here for reprimanding
    Or to eat the fatted calf,
But our souls could take expanding
    And we wouldn't mind a laugh.

Here we are, great king of Glory.
    Now we've found our proper seat.
Pass the plate and tell the story.
    Feels so good to rest our feet.

Faith and the Dry Times

When I'm alone with what my brain believes,
my mouth and throat a ragged thing of words,
my lungs collapsing in a storm of heaves,
my songs all echoes like the mockingbird's,

I call on You, as did your storm-struck men,
to save my confidence that You are near.
Then I lay by ambition, pride, and pen
with satisfaction that my faith is sere.

For only when my life and lips are dry
will I climb up the circling stair toward You
to fall before your feet before I die,
believing as I did before I knew.

Despite the stars sown wide like glowing grains,
we stumble in the dark, yet lose our chains.

The Death of Jesus

The severe anxiety as he prayed the night before
caused his sweat glands to mix blood with sweat.

His skin was fragile when he was flogged
with a whip of leather thongs that contained metal
balls and sharp bones, revealing his spine.

He lost a lot of blood, making him very thirsty.
They raised him on the cross, asphyxiating him.

He died of cardiac arrest.

There is no way
in which he could have survived
to simulate his Resurrection.

5

Canonical Hours

I. Matins (Midnight):

Now is the turn, though still a chill at heart.
If we slept on, the rustle of the rat,
the chitter of the bat, and crying sprites
would be this dark night's voices by default.
On Your behalf, we leave our beds and sing
of light, of healing, of Your fondness for
us foundlings who see none of these as yet.

II. Lauds (Dawn):

World of fuchsia, azure
and a hundred greens—
world of hands and faces.
Every dawn new life,
parable compact
insisting You await,
seated at the table's head,
the candles, torches, hearth,
your face, all lending light,
and we at peace again.

III. Prime (6 a.m.):

In the gruel, in the bread,
every grain Your radiant head.
By our molar grinding of
these we know your tender love.
Thus another way You bring
life to us that we may sing

songs of gratitude and praise
in this world of ice and haze.

IV. Terce (9 a.m.):

When our parents broke your single law,
for our deep flaw
You sentenced one to work and one to pain.
What some will see as bane,
we take as blessing in a harsh disguise.
Though none too wise,
we love the hickory of a handled tool,
the milking stool,
the calluses like honor on our hands,
the sweat that work demands.
On this we focus now instead of birth
and its attendant mirth.

V. Sext (Noon):

Day by day we walk our lifelong path.
The light we prayed for when the world was dark
dazzles all our sight at every noon,
fields aglow like fire and yet uncharred.
Father, teach us to embrace your grace.
Inure our souls that we may bear your love.
Allow these flames, semantic as they are,
to give us, like experience, a taste
for love when we are drowning in its light.

VI. Nones (3 p.m.):

Incomplete, our toil,
heads drip sweat like holy oil.
Now we breathe to God an incense word,
though it seems absurd.

What appears as sloth
gives the soul a cup of broth.
Good, this sacred, brief, mnemonic rest
at the LORD's behest.

VII. Vespers (Sunset):

Now our work afield is done
with the leaving of the sun.
Water purling from each face
glistens like transparent lace.
One who sits apart now reads
words that wisdom writes and heeds.
All we've done and said today
helps us see what prophets say.
Feeding on our simple fare,
every mind's made more aware.
Now our voices rise like smoke
as our unclean tongues invoke
heaven's host to shelter us
from the rays of Hesperus.

VIII. Compline (Bedtime):

Here is the night again,
the bridegroom of the sun now as unreal
as tales that children hear.
But, though we do not see the sun, we've seen
the world by light he's shed.
May we retain a glimmer of that light
behind our lidded eyes
that we may step more safely through our dreams.

www.ingramcontent.com/pod-product-compliance
Lightning Source LLC
LaVergne TN
LVHW021614080426
835510LV00019B/2561